Old GORGIE

by
Malcolm Cant

The house of laughter and figure-8 railway at the Scottish National Exhibition, held at Saughtonhall in 1908.

First published in the United Kingdom, 2002,
by Stenlake Publishing Ltd.
Telephone: 01290 551122
www.stenlake.co.uk

ISBN 1 84033 212 3

The publishers regret that they cannot supply
copies of any pictures featured in this book.

ACKNOWLEDGEMENTS

I would like to acknowledge the assistance of the following people or organisations in lending material (in some cases several years ago) and providing information which has now been used and has greatly enhanced this book: Adult Learning Project; the Aitken family; Jim Andison; Better Gorgie Dalry Campaign; Jack Boyd; Alan Brotchie; Robert J. Bruce; Mrs Anne Campbell on behalf of J. Campbell Harper; Davie Cunningham; Mrs Nellie Denholm; Revd A. Ian Dunlop; Edinburgh Public Libraries; Douglas Garry; Gorgie Mills Bowling Club; the late Wilfred Grubb; the late D. L. G. Hunter; Stanley Jamieson; Betty McKenzie; the late W. McKenzie; Macfarlan Smith Ltd.; Mrs Jean Moffat; James Murie; Jack Paterson; the Salmond family; the Salvation Army; Mrs Pat Scoular; Tynecastle School; United Free Church; Waddie & Co., printers; David Wilson.

The publishers would like to thank Alan Brotchie for providing the pictures featured on pages 4, 27, 41, 46, 47 and the front cover. Those on the front cover and page 25 were taken by the late E. O. Catford.

No self-respecting cook would have been without a copy of *Cox's Manual of Gelatine Cookery*. A leaflet of 'delightful recipes' was enclosed with every packet of Cox's gelatine, which was made at the company's glue works (see page 14) on the south side of Gorgie Road on a site now occupied by Telephone House. The firm was established in Linlithgow in 1725 and moved to Gorgie in 1798, where it remained until its closure in 1969.

INTRODUCTION

In 1995 I wrote and published a book called *Edinburgh: Gorgie and Dalry*. As this is now almost out of print I was very pleased to be asked by Stenlake Publishing to put together two photographic records of the district under the titles *Old Gorgie* and *Old Dalry*. When I first researched these areas some years ago, I gathered a large number of photographs, many of which were never used in the original book. This new publication now gives the opportunity to use these photographs, along with some of the others. The boundary between Gorgie and Dalry has been taken as the Ardmillan junction, but some difficulty has been encountered in allocating pictures in and around Murieston. All I can say is that if your favourite view is not in *Old Gorgie*, perhaps it will be in *Old Dalry*.

Old Gorgie covers the area from Ardmillan westwards to Stenhouse Mansion where the modern district of Stenhouse begins, and includes the various side streets between Gorgie Road and Slateford Road. Historically, Gorgie and its adjacent lands had three substantial houses dating from the seventeenth century: Gorgie House on the north side of Gorgie Road, near Alexander Drive; Stenhouse Mansion at Stenhouse Mill Lane; and Saughton Hall which stood in what is now Saughton Park. By the 1920s Gorgie House was beginning to fall into disrepair and was demolished for the construction of the Poole's Roxy Cinema in 1937. Today, the only one of the three houses to survive is Stenhouse Mansion.

Saughton Hall stood in its own grounds on the north side of Gorgie Road on land now laid out as Saughton Park. The mansion was probably built by Robert Baird, an Edinburgh merchant, after he bought the estate in 1660. During the nineteenth century the house was managed by Dr William Henry Lowe as a mental hospital under the name of Saughton Hall Institute for the Recovery of the Insane. The mansion and its grounds were purchased by Edinburgh Corporation in 1900 for £52,900 and were used for the Scottish National Exhibition of 1908. Unfortunately, Saughton Hall was subsequently allowed to fall into disrepair and was demolished in 1952.

Gorgie's third historic house is the one which has survived to the present day – Stenhouse Mansion – situated on the south side of Gorgie Road almost opposite Stenhouse Drive. Dating from the sixteenth century, the house was greatly improved by Patrick Ellis in 1623 and was sold in 1690 to the Watsons of Saughton. During the nineteenth century the mansion entered a long period of gradual decline which was not effectively arrested until shortly before the outbreak of the Second World War, when it was gifted to the National Trust for Scotland. Fortunately, with the benefit of their care, it is likely to remain in existence for a very long time to come.

While the mansion houses and their large estates were still intact, most of the local population worked on the land. However, during the nineteenth century, Gorgie, like its neighbour Dalry, was subjected to far-reaching developments, not all of which were welcomed by the indigenous population. In the early part of the century the Union Canal was cut through neighbouring land, the Glasgow & Edinburgh Railway opened in 1842, followed by the Caledonian Railway in 1848 and the suburban line in 1884. Even Gorgie Road, between Balgreen and present-day Stewart Terrace, was the subject of several realignments in 1803.

The main build-up in the population of Gorgie occurred in the latter part of the nineteenth century, a little later than in Dalry which was much nearer to the centre of Edinburgh. In the late 1870s, speculative building began along the south side of Gorgie Road at White Park, near to where the Heart of Midlothian Football Club had their first ground. The triangle formed by Henderson Terrace, Angle Park Terrace and Ardmillan Terrace was also under construction with the exception of the site on the corner of Ardmillan Terrace and Angle Park Terrace. At the time this corner was still occupied by the iron church belonging to the first congregation of St Michael's Parish Church. The tenement eventually erected on the site in 1887 has the biblical text 'The Lord Reigneth, Let the Earth Rejoice' on a stone plaque on the west-facing wall. By 1900 houses had been constructed on both sides of Gorgie Road out to about the position of Robertson Avenue, but the area further west was still quite rural.

The population of Gorgie increased substantially as a number of businesses chose to locate further out of town. Among the largest employers, many of whom had previously been in business in other parts of Edinburgh, were: the Caledonian Brewery, 1869; McVitie & Price, biscuits, 1887; the North British Distillery, 1887; Macfarlan Smith, chemicals; and Waddie & Co., printers, 1950. Cox's Glue Works had, of course, been in the district since 1798.

During the First and Second World Wars, many firms in Gorgie turned their attention to the manufacture of items for the war effort but after 1945 the district fell into a long period of partial decline, not seriously halted until the 1980s when organisations such as the Better Gorgie Dalry Campaign were established 'to promote, develop and sustain the economic and physical regeneration of the Gorgie Dalry area. A lot has been achieved, but there is still room for new ideas.

Stenhouse Mansion lies to the south of Gorgie Road almost opposite its junction with Stenhouse Drive. The original building dates from the sixteenth century and was probably built by the Stenhope family. Over the centuries it has had various names, including Saughton Mills and Stenhope Mills, on account of its proximity to an old mill on the Water of Leith. The confusion has been compounded by the variations in the spelling of the family name, Stenhouse, to include Stanehope and Stenhop. In 1623 the mansion was bought by Patrick Eleis, or Ellis, who undertook extensive improvements to the original three-storey, rectangular structure. He doubled the length of the main block southwards and built a new stair-tower and offices projecting from its centre. Ellis also added his 'signature' over the door with his initials P.E., the date 1623, and the words BLISIT BE GOD FOR AL HIS GIFTIS. After several changes of ownership and use, Stenhouse Mansion entered a long period of gradual decline during the nineteenth and early twentieth centuries, to the point where it was semi-derelict by 1929. Fortunately help was at hand, although from an unlikely source. In 1937 the mansion and surrounding land was purchased by the Greyhound Racing Association which constructed a racecourse on the site. Having no use for the dilapidated building, the association gifted it to the National Trust for Scotland which arranged extensive renovation over a period of several years. Thus the present-day condition of the mansion is very much better than as seen in this *c.*1930 photograph.

In *Edinburgh: Gorgie and Dalry* a photograph appeared, dated *c*.1912, showing the shop at 56 Gorgie Road occupied by a Mr Wilson as a newsagents and tobacconists. The caption stated that No. 56 had been the former Tynecastle tollhouse and that it had been demolished for the construction of the Tivoli Cinema. Subsequent research has now shown that this building was not, in fact, the tollhouse. Furthermore, it was not demolished when the cinema was built, as this newly-published photograph illustrates, showing as it does Mr Wilson's shop at No. 56 with part of the Tivoli Cinema on the extreme right.

This photograph is even more interesting than the one above as it shows, on the left, a much more ancient building which is almost certain to have been the tollhouse. The raised area at the front would have allowed the toll-keeper to easily collect tolls from cart or carriage drivers by putting him approximately at eye-level with his customers. These two photographs, which weren't available when *Edinburgh: Gorgie and Dalry* was written, were taken by Nellie Denholm from the window of her flat in a tenement which stood opposite the shop and toll, near the entrance to the present-day Gorgie City Farm. Thanks to her foresight, the uncertainty surrounding Tynecastle Toll has been clarified. In fact neither shop nor tollhouse were demolished until a new row of shops, Nos. 54–64, was built on the site in the 1920s.

The United Free Church of Scotland, Edinburgh West, is on the south side of Gorgie Road a few hundred yards east of the junction with Hutchison Crossway. Its very existence is historically important. When the United Free Church of Scotland merged with the Church of Scotland in 1929 there were several congregations, ministers, elders and members who did not agree with the merger. This dissenting group, known as the United Free Church (Continuing) found themselves with no church buildings and no manses for their ministers. At Gorgie, the United Free congregation met at Ardmillan Hall from 1929 and later moved to Westfield Hall. A few years later its members secured a piece of ground on the south side of Gorgie Road where the present building was erected. The intention was to use the church halls as a place of worship to begin with, and then to construct a bigger church on the front portion of the ground. Unfortunately, funds never became available for the more ambitious building programme and over the years the halls have been progressively adapted as the main place of worship.

North Merchiston Parish Church stood on the south side of Slateford Road, immediately to the west of Shandon Bridge, almost opposite the top of Robertson Avenue. Its congregation was dissolved in 1986 and the building was demolished shortly thereafter. The church's origins, however, can be traced back to the middle of the nineteenth century in the old village of Gorgie where a small religious group met in the Old School building beside Cox's glue works in Gorgie Road. In the mid-1880s the group transferred to a new building, known as the 'Little Church in the Field', on the north side of Gorgie Road. In subsequent years this building was used by other denominations and was later renamed Gorgie War Memorial Hall. Around 1891 a proposal was considered for the erection of another much bigger church on the open ground in front of the Little Church. However, that idea was abandoned in favour of the Slateford Road site where the church seen in this 1904 photograph was opened in 1896.

This photograph of the Little Church in the Field was taken in 1887 shortly after it was built. The old estate wall bordering Gorgie Road can be seen in the foreground and Corstorphine Hill is in the background. The church obviously predates the tenements of Westfield Road and Street. Nowadays the building is used as a community centre, referred to informally as 'Gorgie Mem', a contraction of Gorgie War Memorial Hall.

The Salvation Army has had a considerable visual and spiritual impact on the people of Gorgie and Dalry over a period of many years. When the Gorgie Corps was first established in 1891 that impact was less obvious. In fact the Army's own newspaper, *The War Cry*, devoted only a six-line entry on 12 December to the birth of Edinburgh IV, later referred to as Gorgie Corps, under the command of Captain Maggie Liddle and Lieutenant Cameron. This picture shows the Salvation Army band shortly after it was formed in 1898, outside the Citadel in Murieston Road. Whilst its main purpose is still to accompany the singing at both indoor and outdoor services, the band's range and sphere of activity has been enlarged through regular visits to hospitals, nursing homes, concert halls and Saughton prison. One of its most prestigious engagements was to play on the forecourt of Holyrood Palace for Her Majesty Queen Elizabeth and HRH The Duke of Edinburgh on the occasion of its Diamond Jubilee in July 1958. In 1968 Alex Thain was presented with the Order of the Founder on completing 40 years as bandmaster at Gorgie.

In the early days of the Salvation Army in Gorgie and Dalry, the 'barracks' was a small brick building standing in a field adjoining the Gorgie Road entrance to Tynecastle Park. Its proximity to one of Gorgie's other great attractions ensured that the perimeter fence was used as an unofficial grandstand on Saturday afternoons. Around 1897 the Corps' second home, seen behind these Salvation Army members, was built in Murieston Road. It was a purpose-built citadel of three storeys, including officers' living accommodation. During its 70 years of use the building was gradually developed to accommodate all aspects of the Corps' work. By the 1960s, however, it was clear that new and improved premises were required. The site of Cairns Cottage on the south side of Gorgie Road, near its junction with Hutchison Crossway, was chosen for the new citadel, designed by Matthew, Hamilton, McLean of Edinburgh, and opened by General Coutts in December 1967.

A class of 34 boys and their teacher at Gorgie School, *c*.1913, shortly before the outbreak of the First World War. During the war years, 1914–1918, the headmaster recorded several poignant moments in the daily log:

      4.9.1914. Some male teachers absent as territorials are called up for active service.

      22.1.1915. Mr Ramage left yesterday having joined Kitchener's army.

      18.6.1915. Miss McRury absent all week her brother being amongst those killed at the Dardanelles.

      5.9.1916. Mr Ramage resumed duty having been discharged from the army.

A class of 45 pupils (20 boys and 25 girls) at Gorgie School in Gorgie Road, *c.*1934. Little did they know that within a few years of this relaxed photograph being taken most would be evacuated from Gorgie to Dalkeith and Newtongrange at the outbreak of the Second World War in 1939. Those who did not opt for evacuation were taught in groups of not more than twelve pupils in bowling-green clubhouses, church halls, private houses, and even an air-raid shelter beneath the Roxy Picture House, a few hundred yards from the school gate.

The first Gorgie School was a small low-roofed building in the centre of the old village adjoining Cox's glue works. Gorgie Public School was built in 1871 on a site immediately west of the railway bridge at the junction of Robertson Avenue and Gorgie Road. Its roll rose rapidly, reaching a peak of 1,596 pupils in 1901. However, over the years the number of children attending Gorgie was gradually reduced as other schools were opened nearby: Dalry School in 1878; Dalry Annexe in 1910; Stenhouse School in 1930; Balgreen School in 1934; and Broomhouse School in 1952. Despite the parents' protests, Gorgie School was closed on 31 October 1952, after which the building was used as Tynecastle Annexe until it was demolished in 1993. This photograph was taken in the late 1970s.

Three stalwarts of the Gorgie scene, photographed outside 14 Wardlaw Place in 1931: left, Willie Nisbet; right, Jackie Boyd; centre, Jimmy Nisbet, younger brother of Willie. A little more than a decade after this photograph was taken Jackie Boyd was a fighter pilot during the Second World War.

Tynecastle High School, in McLeod Street, was opened as Tynecastle Supplementary School on 3 September 1912 with fifteen teachers recruited from various Edinburgh schools including Dalry, Gorgie and North Merchiston. More than 500 pupils enrolled, mainly from Craiglockhart School, Dalry School and Gorgie School, but there was insufficient furniture for such a large intake with only twelve classrooms ready for occupation. Despite these initial setbacks the formal opening by the Rt. Hon. Alexander Ure, Lord Advocate, went ahead as planned on 16 November 1912. By 1914 there were 25 classes with an average school roll of 790 pupils. From the very beginning Tynecastle was a new venture for the Edinburgh School Board, concentrating on technical subjects and equipped with all the latest machinery in a range of workshops beside the main building. Subjects taught included joinery, plumbing, cobbling, haircutting, engineering, plastering, laundering, sewing, cooking and housewifery. The academic subjects were taught in the main building where the boys and girls were strictly segregated up to the leaving age of fourteen. These two photographs were probably taken in the first decade of the school's opening. One shows boys in the woodwork room with planes, vices and saws. The other is of girls at the bookkeeping class where an understanding of the double-entry system and an ability to count without a calculator were essential.

Cox's glue works was established at Linlithgow in 1725 but moved within a relatively short period to Bell's Mills at the Dean Village. The firm settled at Gorgie in 1798 where it remained until 1969. For almost two and a half centuries Cox's presence was keenly felt by everyone who lived within breathing space of its strong-smelling processes, one of which can be seen here. Much of Cox's ground on the south side of Gorgie Road was laid out with open pits where the scrows (scrapings from hides and skins) were immersed in water for several weeks at a time. This is what caused the foul smell, especially when the sodden mass was lifted out of the pit to be dried and made ready for the manufacture of glue and gelatine products. The pits were fed from a long lade which was led from the Water of Leith near Saughtonhall and designed to cleanse the scrows of their impurities. A supply of good clean water was so important to the manufacturing process that Mr Cox went to law to protect his interests when the Edinburgh Water Bill was being debated before a Select Committee of the House of Lords in 1856. Counsel was intrigued to know more about the processes and the origins of the skins and hides, but Mr Cox appears to have been equal to him in caustic wit.

    Counsel: We have been told that you use dead cat skins and dead dog skins. Are these articles of common use?

    Mr Cox: I have never heard of them. I have heard of them going to pie shops but that is all.

Paterson's joinery business was started by James Paterson *c.*1868 at the rear of the cottage known as Glenlea in Gorgie Road, a few yards east of the United Free Church. James's son David came into the business in 1893 and in turn was succeeded by his two sons, David Jnr. in 1922 and Jack in 1927. The business was relocated in 1934 to much larger premises on the corner of Gorgie Road and Hutchison Crossway. This photograph, taken at Glenlea in 1912, shows David Paterson Snr. on the left and Joe Malcolm on the right. The horizontal bar projecting from the vertical post at the lower right-hand corner of the picture was used to hold wheels while they were painted. In the days of horse-drawn carts, the Patersons were heavily involved in the skilled job of making and repairing wooden-spoked wheels. The hub, or nave as it was called, was made of elm. The spokes were of oak and the felloes (forming the outer circumference) were made of either ash or elm. It was a skilled job to fit the spokes and shape the felloes using a trainer, or measuring device, from the centre of the hub. Once assembled, using Cox's glue, wheels were taken to McDougall the blacksmith to have an iron rim fitted.

This room, full of complicated machinery, was the die stamping department of Waddie & Co. Ltd., printers, in Slateford Road in 1960. The firm was established in 1860 by the brothers John and Charles Waddie at 11 Waterloo Place. After a spell at Queen Street and St Stephen Street, Waddie's moved to Slateford Road in 1950 to premises previously used by Simon Henderson, the baker. Further expansion saw a purpose-built factory opened in Livingston in 1987 where the entire workforce was based after closure of the Slateford Road premises in 2000.

Macfarlan Smith Ltd., manufacturer of fine chemicals and natural extracts, occupies the extensive Blandfield works situated within the triangle of land between the railway lines at the north end of Wheatfield Road. The company's position as a leading manufacturer of specialised products for the medical profession is the culmination of a long association with the pharmaceutical industry in Edinburgh. Its roots go back to the late eighteenth century and include world-famous names such as J. F. Macfarlan; Duncan, Flockhart & Co.; and T. & H. Smith. This picture shows the Blandfield chemical works at Gorgie, the name Blandfield having been taken from the previous works in Lower Broughton Road.

The oldest part of the trio is probably J. F. Macfarlan, who was in business as a druggist at 139 High Street as early as 1815 and took over another firm which dated back to 1777. The second oldest, Duncan, Flockhart & Co., supplied the chloroform for Dr Simpson's historic experiment into anaesthesia on 4 November 1847. Its factory and laboratories were, for many years, at Holyrood Road almost opposite the site of the Scottish Parliament building. In 1952 Duncan, Flockhart & Co. were acquired by T. & H. Smith Ltd., who began at Duke Street, moved to Canonmills and then relocated to the Gorgie premises in 1906. The trio came together in 1960 to form Macfarlan Smith Ltd., which was taken over by Glaxo in 1963. Finally, a management buyout bought Macfarlan Smith from Glaxo in 1990. The offices in this picture can be seen at the right-hand edge of the aerial view above. (Both photographs come from *A History of T. & H. Smith*, published in 1952.)

Shortly after 7.00 a.m. on 1 May 1908 His Royal Highness Prince Arthur of Connaught arrived at Waverley station where he was met by Sir Robert Cranston (former Lord Provost of Edinburgh), chairman of the executive committee of the Scottish National Exhibition. Prince Arthur had travelled overnight from London to be in Edinburgh to open the exhibition at Saughton Hall on the outskirts of the city. A grand lunch for 300 guests was held at the North British Station Hotel (now the Balmoral), after which the entourage made its way out to Saughton Hall for the official opening at 3.00 p.m. After the Prince had declared the exhibition open, Lord Provost James P. Gibson announced that the event had already got off to a very good start as the anticipated overdraft of £16,000 had been replaced by a bank balance of £780. The Prince's tour of the exhibits would have taken him along the Royal Promenade, seen in this photograph, to the various semi-permanent exhibition halls and smaller sideshows and places of entertainment. The unusual rocky exhibit on the right of the picture was, appropriately, by Alex Ferguson, confectioners since 1822 and manufacturers of Edinburgh Rock.

The exhibition was laid out on the garden ground of Saughton Hall Mansion to the west of Balgreen Road on land now used as Saughton rose garden and public park. This provided an enormous amount of space for the main exhibits, with room for a number of places of popular entertainment on the west side of the site. The two most popular features were the water chute, seen here, and the figure-8 railway, built by T. M. Hartin & Co. of Pittsburgh, USA. These two attractions and the various tournaments, pageants, displays and balloon ascents all contributed to excellent daily attendances. More than 125,000 people visited the exhibition on the opening day, and by the time it closed on 31 October the total number had reached 3.5 million. On the last day there were 53,563 attendances, a number of whom decided to have their own grand finale immediately after the formal closing by Sir Robert Cranston. Owing to an earlier disturbance at the Theatre Bar the decision had been taken to close the bar early, a move which infuriated the crowd to the point where the police had to be called to restore order. At the bandstand where things were reaching a crescendo, policemen, perhaps unaccustomed to the change in beat, were forced to raise their batons as youths pitched in with chairs and music stands.

At its north end, the Royal Promenade opened onto a rectangular arena bounded by the main buildings of the exhibition, all designed by the architects Walker & Ramsay of Glasgow and built of timber and white fibrous plaster. These comprised the industrial hall (illustrated here); the club; the machinery hall; the concert hall; the fine art building; and Canada House. The exhibition attracted a wide variety of participants, with applications for sites being received from France, Italy, Denmark, Holland, Russia, Serbia, Persia, Japan, China, the United States of America and Canada. By far the largest covered area was the 100,000 square foot industrial hall or palace of industries. Second to that was the machinery hall with exhibits pertaining to shipping, mining, gas, steam, electricity, water, sewage, baking and printing.

THE VEGETARIAN RESTAURANT (Near Water Chute) **SIXPENNY MEALS**
EDINBURGH NATIONAL EXHIBITION.

The vegetarian restaurant, no doubt a novelty in 1908 with its sixpenny meals, was located near the water chute. There is no record of how popular it was but it would have faced competition from the wide variety of cuisine on offer, including the tearoom with its scones and pancakes and Van Houten's cocoa pavilion, where cocoa was available at a penny per cup including a biscuit.

John McBain, photographed on what appears to be a special family outing, in charge of his pony and trap (with the family dog between the wheels) outside the gates of Saughton Park. The bridge over the Water of Leith was erected at the time of the Scottish National Exhibition in 1908.

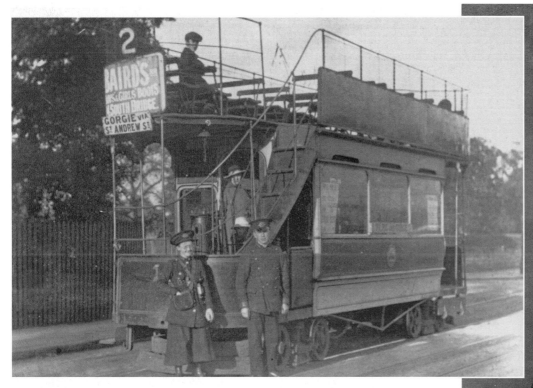

Conductress Helen Andison and her driver at Saughton cable car terminus, near Ford's Road, *c*.1918. The advertisement on the front of the tram is for Baird's Boys' and Girls' Boots.

Helen Andison (née Hutcheon) photographed *c*.1918 when she was 35 years of age. Helen was a conductress on cable car service 2, which ran through the districts of Dalry and Gorgie to the terminus near Ford's Road. She was employed during the years of the First World War only, as she was required to resign from her job at the end of the war to allow male workers to return to their jobs after demobilisation.

Cable car No. 107 on service 2 travelling west on Gorgie Road, *c*.1912. The high wall on the right is at the Magdalene Asylum, now Springwell House. This picture shows once again the small shop featured on page 5. The site between the shop and the tenement, fronted here by billboards, was used for the construction of the Tivoli Cinema (in its first incarnation) in 1913.

An elegant electric tram car operating service No. 3 on the new bridge over the Water of Leith at Chesser.

Electric tram car No. 189 on service 4 travels west along Slateford Road near Gorgie station in 1953. The destination board 'Piershill' is incorrect (it had probably been altered by the driver prior to reaching the terminus) as the car is clearly going west to the terminus at the south end of Chesser Avenue. The advertisement is for 'Weston's Quality Biscuits – save pence per pound'. To the left of the tramcar is a sign reading 'British Railways – Gorgie East, Passenger & Goods Station' beside the small roadway which ran down to the station on the suburban line and also to the marshalling yards. The corner building with the conical roof to the right of the tram was at the time the head office of T. & J. Bernard's Edinburgh Brewery, which extended behind the tenements on the west side of Robertson Avenue.

An electric tram car photographed on service 4 in Slateford Road near the junction with Merchiston Grove. This time the destination board 'Piershill' is correct. The advertisement is again for Weston's Biscuits, and judging by the pennants flying from the trolley cable this could have been Coronation year, 1953, although pennants were also used on other occasions, notably during the Edinburgh International Festival. The unusual arrangement of the rails in the foreground, known as interlaced track, was devised to allow the tram to pass any brewer's lorry at the Caledonian Brewery (which can be seen on the right of the picture). Also on the right, in the middle distance, is the pedimented roofline of the Lyceum Picture House which was opened at the top of Robertson Avenue in 1926 and closed in 1961. On the left is Ivy Terrace, part of the Slateford colonies, which include the street names Laurel, Violet, Primrose and Myrtle. The shop on the corner of Merchiston Grove is that of E. Renton & Son, bakers and confectioners.

The Royal Train, in the livery of the Caledonian Railway, at Gorgie sidings in 1914 with Peter Murie second from the right. The existence of a Royal Train dates back to 13 June 1842 when the engine *Phlegethon*, pulling the royal saloon and six other carriages, transported Queen Victoria from Slough to Paddington. Isambard Kingdom Brunel, the great nineteenth century engineer, accompanied Queen Victoria on this inaugural journey. Modern Royal Train rolling stock consists of eight purpose-built saloons and two Royal Class 47 diesel locomotives, *Prince William* and *Prince Henry*, assembled in different combinations according to the requirements of the journey and the number of people travelling. In 2000–2001 the total cost of the Royal Train was £596,000. During that period it made seventeen journeys.

Gorgie station was on the suburban line, a few hundred yards north of Slateford Road which crosses the line via the bridge seen in the background of this picture. The station could be reached from both Slateford Road and a narrow road running southwards from Gorgie Road. Much of the early planning of the suburban line was done by Sir Thomas Bouch, designer of the ill-fated Tay Bridge which collapsed with the loss of many lives on 28 December 1879. After the Tay Bridge disaster, Bouch was relieved of his commission on the suburban line and the final survey was undertaken by George Trimble of Trimble & Peddie. The line was opened in 1884. This picture shows locomotive No. 65243, a Class J36 0-6-0.

Locomotive No. 61222, a Class B1 4-6-0, pulls out of Gorgie station with its train to travel southwards to Craiglockhart, Morningside, Blackford and Newington. To the right of the picture is T. & J. Bernard's Edinburgh Brewery which had a siding communicating with the suburban line a few hundred yards to the north of the station.

This view looking east (towards the city centre) is taken from the Chesser Avenue end of the Gorgie sidings which were used for the daily transportation of cattle and sheep in semi-open wagons to the slaughterhouses at Chesser. The sidings and cattle docks were constructed under the direction of Blyth & Westland, civil engineers, to provide a frontage of 3,600 feet capable of taking 200 wagons at a time. The largest area of the complex was given over to the slaughterhouses, which could deal annually with 28,000 cattle, 8,000 swine, 4,500 calves and 178,000 sheep. Each part of the slaughterhouse had its own special function including the killing and cooling halls, tripery, dung house, fat searching house, boiler house and condemned meat plant. In addition to the many people employed in the slaughterhouses, the processes sustained many other businesses, including tanning, leatherworks, glue-making and many small family butchers.

A 1932 photograph of J. McKenzie, dry-salters, on the corner of Gorgie Road and McLeod Street (according to the ninth edition of the *Concise Oxford Dictionary*, a dry-salter was 'a dealer in dyes, gums, drugs, oils, pickles, tinned meats, etc.'). Here the window display is dominated by advertising for One-O-One ('Cleans Without Scratching'), a miracle cleaning product that cost sixpence per canister. Only two other products are visible: Swift floor and lino polish and the famous 'Tapwata', a wallpaper adhesive whose only additive was apparent to even the most inexperienced home decorator.

J. Mitchell's combined hairdressers and tobacconists was situated at 267 Gorgie Road, on the south side of the road near its junction with Robertson Avenue. When this photograph was taken the window display was devoted entirely to *Smart Fiction*. This weekly periodical was published in London between 1913 and 1924 and ran to 614 issues before being incorporated into *Smart Novels*. The issue prominently displayed in the window bears the legend 'The World of Sin', while billboards advertise other sensational sounding stories including 'Her Honour at Stake' and 'The Soul of an Outcast'.

The large corner premises at 90 Gorgie Road, on the east corner with McLeod Street, were occupied in 1932 by J. McKenzie, manufacturing tinsmith and general ironmonger. The windows, doorway and shop floor were crammed with all manner of household items: brushes, baskets, garden poles, cut leather and straps, Persil washing powder, stepladders and carpet beaters. Many years ago the tenement containing this shop became unsafe and was demolished. The site is now occupied by a small playground for children.

In 1919 Gilbert F. Nicolson formed the Edinburgh Bainfield Football Club which took its name from its home ground opposite what was formerly the house of Bainfield on the south side of Dundee Street. The Bainfield club won the Walker and Cowan cups in the Juvenile League during the season 1920–21. Despite the promising start, and the comparative youth of the winning team (pictured here), a decision was taken in 1924 to switch the main allegiance of the club from football to bowls. The first clubhouse for Bainfield Bowling and Recreation Club was at Harrison Park. After many years of deliberation, the club (renamed Bainfield Bowling and Social Club in 1947) secured its own ground in 1951 by purchasing land from Edinburgh Corporation on the east side of Hutcheson Crossway. It has remained there ever since and has rebuilt and enlarged the premises on more than one occasion. The individuals featured here are:

Back row: J. Allison, R. McKay, A. Nisbet, J. Berrie
Third row: A. Strachan, J. Bulmer, W. Hay, D. Stewart, W. King, G. Edwards, A. Manzie (trainer)
Second row: J. McKay (president), W. McKenzie, J. McKay (captain), G. McNicol, G. Nicolson (secretary), W. Manzie (treasurer)
Front: W. Greenhill, W. McKay.

This photograph shows the Heart of Midlothian v Motherwell in 1954, an era which many supporters still regard as one of the team's finest, with Conn, Wardhaugh and Bauld firmly established as the 'Terrible Trio'. The Heart of Midlothian Football Club was founded in 1874 by a group of young footballers whose other Saturday passion was attending the Heart of Mid-lothian dance hall, which was near the present-day high-rise flats in Dumbiedykes Road. When the club first started, it played on the Meadows along with several others including its arch-rival, Hibernian. Hearts had its own ground at Powburn and then Powderhall before moving to Gorgie in 1881. The first ground, on the site of present-day Wardlaw Street and Wardlaw Place, was opened on 9 April 1881. The club moved over the road to its present ground on 10 April 1886.

This picture shows the old clubhouse of Gorgie Mills Bowling Club in Alexander Drive, with those club-members who had won the Water of Leith League, Riddle Trophy in 1937. Although the club still exists, the origin of the name Gorgie Mills is beginning to be less well-known. The club was started on 20 June 1904 following a challenge match between the glue and gelatine departments of J. & G. Cox Ltd. of Gorgie Mills. At that time, Cox's works was a thriving concern which had made its presence known in the area for many years on account of the pungent odour emitted during its manufacturing processes. Thanks to a gift of £1,000 from Cox's management, the green was constructed quickly and was ready for the opening on 20 May 1905. The close link between the firm and the club was maintained even after ownership of J. & G. Cox was transferred to Bryant & May. Unfortunately, in 1969, Bryant & May announced the closure of Cox's Gorgie Mills factory but the club purchased the green and clubhouse for £5,000 and has successfully maintained its independence to the present day. The photograph shows, left to right:

Back row: R. Linn; J. Donaldson; J. Galloway; W. Burt JP, Pres.; W. C. Robertson; R. Paterson; W. Burnett; D. S. Donaldson.
Front row: J. Westwood; W. Tait; L. Fender Jr.; W. Brown; H. Wallace; E. Alston; A. Sibbald; L. Fender Sr.

This photograph was taken in 1952 looking east from the railway bridge carrying the suburban line over Gorgie Road. The entrance to Robertson Avenue can be seen on the right, with Wheatfield Road, leading to the North British Distillery, on the left. The premises on the corner of Wheatfield Road and Gorgie Road are occupied by the Clydesdale & North of Scotland Bank, whose manager at the time was J. C. McCulloch. Other premises between the bank and the electric tram car include: Elliot & Stuart, upholsterers at No. 302; D. Accettola, hairdresser at No. 292; and the Tynecastle Billiard Saloon at No. 274. The Gorgie Hairdressing Saloon, shown on page 32, stood on the opposite side of the road near the junction with Robertson Avenue.

Wheatfield Road, Gorgie, Edinburgh. 340/589

Wheatfield Road looking north, probably in the 1930s when most traffic was still horse-drawn. The cart on the right belonged to R. D. Galloway, coal merchant and contractor of 10 Stewart Terrace. Its tailboard announces that coal is 'sold by ton or cwt [hundredweight]'. The cart in the centre is loaded with two barrels and could perhaps have been going to the North British Distillery, which can be seen at the far end of Wheatfield Road. The North British Distillery Co. Ltd. was incorporated on 24 October 1885, the main backers being John M. Crabbie, William Sanderson and Andrew Usher, all of whom already had many years experience in the whisky trade. The premises at Gorgie were built in record time by the Glasgow engineers Russell & Spence for the sum of £142,000. By 20 September 1887 the first managing director, William Sanderson, was able to send out samples of grain whisky to the trade, commenting that 'in no circumstances whatever shall we admit within the gates of this distillery any inferior material', a pledge which they have maintained to the present day.

Cattle being herded into the slaughterhouses on the west side of Chesser Avenue. Public slaughterhouses were first established in Edinburgh by the Edinburgh Slaughterhouses Act of 1850. The purpose of the Act was to protect the public by regulating the standards of hygiene required in slaughtering animals for public consumption. Up until the beginning of the twentieth century, slaughterhouses and markets were located in several densely populated areas of Edinburgh, notably at Fountainbridge and Lauriston Place. Following a number of studies in 1902, Edinburgh Town Council, as governors of Trinity Hospital, feued 25 acres of ground at Gorgie for new slaughterhouses and meat markets. In addition to the main building costs of £100,000, a sum of £7,000 was included for the construction of Chesser Avenue and the bridges over the railway. The substantial building with the pedimented roofline on the left of the picture is St Cuthbert's Co-operative laundry, which was opened in 1916 at a cost of £20,000. Until the end of the First World War in 1918 it was heavily committed to army contracts.

GORGIE CAR TERMINUS, EDINBURGH. 340/579.

Looking east (towards the city centre) on Gorgie Road near its junction with Chesser Avenue, which can be seen on the right. The building with the light-coloured gable wall to the right of the tramcar forms part of the old hamlet of Delhaig, dating from the end of the nineteenth century. It seems likely that the houses of Delhaig would have been occupied by farm labourers working on the adjacent Gorgie farm, or perhaps workers from Saughton leatherworks on the other side of Gorgie Road. The church building on the right of the picture, Edgar Hall, is named after the Edgar family who financed its construction in 1912. In 1935 a larger church, Stenhouse Saughton, was built on the vacant plot where the timber gate is. The new church was designed by T. Aitken Swan and the foundation stone was laid by the Duke of Kent, Lord High Commissioner. The congregation of Stenhouse Saughton was linked with St Aidan's in 1983 and a full union of the two congregations took place in 1993.

In 1905 the south-west corner of Westfield Road and Gorgie Road still retained a certain old-world charm, with mature trees and the estate wall still intact. The building on the left is part of Gorgie Crescent and the high chimney in the background is that of the Pentland Laundry, the site now occupied by the B&Q store in Stevenson Road.

Looking north along Westfield Road *c.*1912. According to *The Place Names of Edinburgh* by Stuart Harris, the position of Westfield Road is of great antiquity, being shown in substantially the same alignment on Roy's map of 1753 and leading to Damhead, Roseburn and Coltbridge. The north end of the road was known as Damhead Road and the remainder called Coltbridge Road until 1899 when it all became Westfield Road. The shop on the right-hand corner is occupied by James Summers & Sons, bakers and confectioners at 346 Gorgie Road, the bakehouse being in Murieston Lane. On the left of the picture the long wall marks the boundary of Gorgie Crescent which is shown in more detail overleaf.

In 1904 these very distinctive houses with projecting windows and outside stairs formed part of Gorgie Crescent, which lay between Alexander Drive and Westfield Road. Originally the crescent was reached directly from Gorgie Road but that entrance was blocked off by the construction of the flats and shops (with the projecting balconies) which were built on Gorgie Road in 1925. Many of the occupants of Gorgie Crescent worked nearby at Cox's glue works.

Many local children have turned out for the cameraman in this 1912 photograph, taken at the junction of Wardlaw Place (left) and Wardlaw Terrace (right). Large families meant that small local traders were able to make a reasonable living as grocers or confectioners, even in locations quite far from the main shopping streets of Gorgie Road and, to a lesser extent, Slateford Road. One such shop is sandwiched into the unusual gap between the tenement buildings on the right.

As the main shopping area in the mid-1950s, the hustle and bustle of Gorgie Road is evident in this photograph looking east towards the city centre. The tenement building protruding into the road near the railway bridge sat at the junction with McLeod Street and is referred to on page 33. On the right of the picture are: Nu-Pin Cleaners at No. 127 on the corner of Newton Street; W. Armstrong Sinclair, painter and decorator at No. 125; and Alice Heaney, confectioner, at No. 123. Among the many shops on the left are: J. Lorimer the butcher at 112a; Redpath Radio, wireless specialists at 110a; and nearer to McLeod Street, Glass's Fruit Market and McPherson the fishmonger. The Gorgie railway bridge, decorated with iron garlands, was built *c.*1860.

For many years this bold notice – 'British Railways Gorgie East Passenger & Goods Station' – adorned the bridge carrying the suburban line over Gorgie Road. Beyond the bridge, where the light is stronger, are the junctions of Wheatfield Road (left) and Robertson Avenue (right). Nearer to the camera, the small opening on the right leads to Gorgie station and the various marshalling yards from which several Edinburgh coal merchants operated. The station could also be reached from Slateford Road. The large advertisement on the left bridge buttress is for Andrew's Liver Salts, with a poster for Player's Navy Cut cigarettes ('Ever Dependable') on the right.

The picture postcard from which this view has been reproduced was posted on 8 September 1914, the sender commenting to the recipient in Dublin that there is a 'keen east wind here – have a muffler on'. It is not clear whether the comment means that the sender is wearing a muffler or recommending the use of one in event of the recipient visiting Edinburgh. Since the photograph was taken the street scene has changed greatly, but not the weather! The photograph looks down Ardmillan Terrace with Angle Park Terrace on the right. The corner shop at 25 Ardmillan Terrace is that of George King, family grocer and coal agent, who lived round the corner at 67 Angle Park Terrace. One of the very early open-topped electric trams can be seen in the middle distance. The group of well-dressed men on the left could be either the chief mourners or a group of undertakers outside North Merchiston Cemetery. The cemetery was first laid out in 1874 as New Dalry Cemetery but changed its name to North Merchiston Cemetery in the mid-1880s.

In this comparatively modern picture, the electric tramway system has been replaced by buses and the terminus for service No. 4 has been extended from Slateford to Oxgangs. The bus is on Slateford Road with Ashley Terrace to the right. Just out of shot to the left is the Caledonian Brewery, while the near end of the bridge parapet on the right abuts North Merchiston Church, seen on page 7.

Nine girls of various ages line up for the curtain opening at one of Gorgie's greatest shows – with a truly international flavour – the Smithfield Street back green concert of 1951. These informal shows were put on for special events such as the Coronation and other royal occasions, and also during the long summer holidays. Costumes and props were begged or borrowed from mothers, aunties, grannies and friendly neighbours. From left to right, wearing different national costumes, those featured are: Helen Hood (Spain); Christine Law (USA); Brenda (Turkey); Morag Cameron (Ireland); Harriet Hood, sister of Helen (Holland); Pat Sharp (wearing Indian [Native American] dress); Sheila Bain (Japan); Margaret Liddell (China); Maureen Jolly (Scotland).